This book belongs to

_____

A
Stirring Sip
of Chicken Soup
for the Soul®

Uplifting Moments
from Everyday
Heroes

**Andrews McMeel
Publishing**

Kansas City

ISBN: 0-8362-5089-3

A
Stirring Sip
of Chicken Soup
for the Soul®

Uplifting Moments
from Everyday
Heroes

Inspired by the #1 New York Times bestseller

by Jack Canfield and Mark Victor Hansen

Courage in a Fire

by Barbara A. Lewis

*M*elinda Clark pulled the blanket up under Courtney's chin and whispered, "Good night, Corky." It was 10:00 P.M. and time for bed. Melinda grinned and patted the huge lump under the covers created by Courtney's three-foot panda. The two sisters shared the same room, but thirteen-year-old Melinda didn't mind at all. Courtney, who was only four, seemed like her baby, too.

Melinda jumped under her own covers, but she didn't pull them up. Even though it was February and there was snow frozen on the ground outside, it seemed unusually warm that night, especially for Everett, Pennsylvania.

Something wet slopped along her cheek. "Oh, Beau. You're a good dog." The miniature collie licked her again. His tail thumped alongside her bed and she rubbed his sable fur.

Melinda's nose twitched at the smoky odor in the air. It was probably just the wood stove downstairs. Fumes traveled up the staircase easily. Melinda shut her eyes.

Two-year-old Justin startled her as he burst through the doorway. He ran over to Melinda's bed and banged his fists on her. "Mom hurt!" His face flushed red.

"What?" Melinda jumped up. The carpet felt very warm as she dropped her bare feet onto the floor. The smoky smell was stronger as she stood up.

What was going on? She rubbed her tingling cheeks and ran into the hall between the two second-story bedrooms. She paused. As she opened the door at the top of the stairs, smoke sucked up the steps in swirls. Orange flames crackled and leaped toward her like snatching fingers. She covered her hot face and screamed.

"Wayne!" She turned and yelled for her twelve-year-old brother. Although his bedroom light was on, she couldn't even see his bed through the ballooning smoke. But Wayne fought through the gray haze and stumbled into her. He was in his underwear.

"My window!" Melinda yelled.

Together they ran into Melinda's room to the double windows, where Wayne began struggling with the stubborn latch on the chest-high ledge.

"Pull! Shove it."

"I'm yanking!"

The fiberglass curtains melted down the

sides of the window. Flecks of hot plastic burned into Wayne's bare back.

Melinda smashed her fist against the latch. If they couldn't get it open, they were going to die...

Wayne banged at the latch, too.

Suddenly it budged, then slipped open. But as they shoved on the window, it held tightly shut, swollen from the waves of heat.

Melinda's eyes stung. She gritted her teeth. They weren't going to die from these flames! "Shove, Wayne! Together! Now!" They banged on the window. "Again! Harder!" She coughed. She threw all her 100 pounds behind the thrust.

Wayne shoved, too, and together they finally forced the stubborn window open.

Melinda told Wayne to climb out on the

plastic porch roof. She handed Courtney over the window. Then Melinda pulled herself over the window ledge.

The three children walked to the edge of the roof, looking for a way down. Wayne jumped to the ground to catch the younger kids.

Suddenly Melinda looked at Wayne, her eyes round circles. "Justin. Where's Justin? Justin!" She screamed. He had been right with them!

Without pausing for breath, she turned around and climbed back over the hot window ledge.

"Justin!" she called.

She dropped onto her hands and knees and crawled low on the hot carpet. She found the closet and felt her hands around.

No Justin. She tried to call, but she choked. Her throat felt like hot coals. Yanking on the tangled nightie under her burning knees, she bumped into Courtney's five-foot-tall toy dog and duck, knocking them both over.

Could Justin have gone back into his bedroom? If he had, she'd never make it through the smoke and flames, which now sucked up the open staircase and window as if a vacuum were outside the window.

Stretching out flat, she felt under Courtney's bed. No Justin.

She coughed in spasms and grabbed at her throat. She couldn't breathe. She wasn't going to make it.

As she crawled toward the window she heard a noise coming from under her bed. She scrambled across the floor and reached underneath the bed, her hand bumping into fur. Beau. He whimpered again and licked her hand. She searched her fingers past Beau and touched hair. Justin. He was there hiding, too. *Thanks for whimpering, Beau,* she thought.

She grabbed Justin by his hair and pulled him out. He clung to her like a baby koala as she crawled back toward the window.

She lifted him over the window ledge and climbed out behind, gasping for mouthfuls of air. But as she stepped onto the plastic roof, her foot crashed through melting plastic up to her knee. She ripped her leg out of the hole and moved to the edge of the roof.

A second later, the picture window below them exploded. Shattering glass flew out thirty feet. Courtney and Justin screamed and pulled at Melinda's arms.

"Beau!" Melinda yelled. She looked behind at the flames licking out the bedroom window. "Oh, Beau!" She tried to swallow, and without another pause, she pushed both younger children off the roof and into the snow eighteen feet below. She leaped behind them, practically smashing Justin as she hit the ground.

A trooper who had seen the fire from the road scooped up the children and carried them across the glass and snow to his car.

"Mommy!" Justin cried.

"Where's Mom?" Melinda asked. She ran up to the neighbor's porch just as her mom ran across the snow to wrap Melinda in her arms. "I was calling 911," she choked, as she grabbed Wayne in a hug. "I was down in the basement changing the wash. I saw you at the top of the stairs. I yelled at you to get out."

The trooper carried the little ones into the neighbor's house. They called their dad, who was working the night shift at Everite Door Manufacturing.

Melinda dropped onto a beanbag chair. The voices and faces swirled around her. She passed out for a few moments. When she came to, she was in an ambulance. The red light flashed. The siren screamed. She drifted in and out of consciousness several more times before reaching the hospital.

Melinda was treated for smoke inhalation, as were her brothers and sister. Melinda's nightgown was melted in spots and although it stuck to her skin, her body beneath it wasn't burned.

Both she and Wayne suffered minor burns, however. Melinda's leg was scratched and burned from where it had broken through the roof, while Wayne's back was burned in small spots from the fiberglass curtains. Courtney and Justin received scratches in their tumble from the overhang. Their pajamas were scorched. But all four children were alive.

Justin kept repeating, "An angel picked me up and threw me out the window. It was a real angel. I know it."

Melinda smiled. She hugged Justin and closed her eyes.

No one could determine the cause of the fire.

"It wasn't until the next day when we

went back that I got really scared," Melinda remembers. "When we walked into the downstairs, it was really strange. Some things were burned, and others weren't. Like the fish was still alive, swimming in his bowl in the dining room. But our bedrooms were ruined."

Her brown eyes suddenly filled with tears. "Beau didn't make it." She looked down. "I had to leave him under my bed."

But Justin did make it because Melinda crawled back into the flames to save her brother. Her fast action and courage wouldn't let her give up. She was an angel, indeed.

A Very Belated Thank You

by Laurie Pines

*W*hen my son, Mark, was in the third grade, he saved all his allowance for over two months to buy holiday presents for those he loved. He had saved twenty dollars. The third Saturday in December, Mark announced that he had made his list and had his money in his pocket.

I drove him to a local drugstore, the modern version of what we used to call the five-and-dime. Mark picked up a hand basket and went off on his own, while I waited patiently reading a book at the front of the store. It took Mark over forty-five minutes to pick out his presents. The smile on his face as he approached the checkout counter was truly joyful. The clerk rang up his purchases as I politely looked the other way. Mark kept within his budget and reached into his pocket for his money. It was not there. There was a hole in his pocket, but no money. Mark stood in the middle of the store holding his basket, tears rolling down his cheeks. His whole body was shaking with his sobs. Then an amazing thing happened. A customer in the store came up to Mark. She knelt down to his level and took him in her arms and said, "You would do me the greatest favor if you let me replace your money. It would be the most wonderful present you could ever give me. I only ask that one day, you pass it on. One day, when you are grown, I would like you to find someone you can help. When you do help this other person, I know you will feel as good about it as I do now." Mark took the money, tried to dry his tears and ran to the checkout counter as fast as he could go. I think we all enjoyed our gifts that year almost as much as Mark enjoyed giving them to us.

I would like to say thank you to that incredible woman. I would like to tell her that four years later, Mark went house to house collecting blankets and coats for the people in the Oakland fire — and he thought of her. I would like to tell her that every time I give food to a homeless family, I think of her. And I want to promise her that Mark will never forget to keep passing it on.

"We're All Here to Learn"

by Charles Slack
As told by Bessie Pender

"**S**ixteen," I said. I have forgotten the math question my second-grade teacher, Joyce Cooper, asked that day, but I will never forget my answer. As soon as the number left my mouth, the whole class at Smallwood Elementary School in Norfolk, Virginia, started laughing. I felt like the stupidest person in the world.

Mrs. Cooper fixed them with a stern look. Then she said, "We're all here to learn."

Another time, Mrs. Cooper asked us to write a report about what we hoped to do with our lives. I wrote, "I want to be a teacher like Mrs. Cooper."

She wrote on my report, "You would make an outstanding teacher because you are determined and you try hard." I was to carry those words in my heart for the next twenty-seven years.

After I graduated from high school in 1976, I married a wonderful man, Ben, a mechanic. Before long, Latonya was born.

We needed every dime just to get by. College—and teaching—was out of the question. I did, however, wind up with a job in a school — as a janitor's assistant. I cleaned seventeen classrooms at Larrymore Elementary School each day, including Mrs. Cooper's. She had transferred to Larrymore after Smallwood closed down.

I would tell Mrs. Cooper that I still wanted to teach, and she would repeat the words she had written on my report years earlier. But bills always seemed to get in the way.

Then one day in 1986 I thought of my dream, of how badly I wanted to help children. But to do that I needed to arrive in the mornings as a teacher — not in the afternoons to mop up.

I talked it over with Ben and Latonya, and it was settled: I would enroll at Old Dominion University. For seven years I attended classes in the mornings before work. When I got home from work, I studied. On days I had no classes to attend, I worked as a teaching assistant for Mrs. Cooper.

Sometimes I wondered whether I had the strength to make it. When I got my first failing grade, I talked about quitting. My younger sister Helen refused to hear it. "You want to be a teacher," she said. "If you stop, you'll never reach your dream."

Helen knew about not giving up — she'd been fighting diabetes. When either of us got down, she would say, "You're going to make it. We're going to make it."

In 1987, Helen, only twenty-four, died of kidney failure related to diabetes. It was up to me to make it for both of us.

On May 8, 1993, my dream day arrived — graduation. Getting my college degree and state teaching license officially qualified me to be a teacher.

I interviewed with three schools. At Coleman Place Elementary School, principal Jeanne Tomlinson said, "Your face looks so familiar." She had worked at Larrymore more than ten years earlier. I had cleaned her room, and she remembered me.

Still, I had no concrete offers. The call came when I had just signed my eighteenth contract as a janitor's assistant. Coleman Place had a job for me teaching fifth grade.

Not long after I started, something happened that brought the past rushing back. I had written a sentence full of grammatical errors on the blackboard. Then I asked students to come and correct the mistakes.

One girl got halfway through, became confused and stopped. As the other children laughed, tears rolled down her cheeks. I gave her a hug and told her to get a drink of water. Then, remembering Mrs. Cooper, I fixed the rest of the class with a firm look. "We're all here to learn," I said.

Not a One!

by Dave Galloway

*L*ittle Chad was a shy, quiet young man. One day he came home and told his mother that he'd like to make a valentine for everyone in his class. Her heart sank. She thought, *I wish he wouldn't do that!* because she had watched the children when they walked home from school. They laughed and hung onto each other and talked to each other. But Chad was never included. Nevertheless, she decided she would go along with her son. So she purchased the paper and glue and crayons. Night after night, Chad painstakingly made thirty-five valentines.

Valentine's Day dawned, and Chad was beside himself with excitement. He carefully stacked them up, put them in a bag, and bolted out the door. His mother decided to bake him his favorite cookies and serve them nice and warm with a cool glass of milk when he came home from school. She just knew he would be disappointed, and maybe that would ease the pain a little. It hurt her to think that he wouldn't get many valentines—maybe none at all.

That afternoon she had the cookies and milk on the table. When she heard the children outside, she looked out the window. Sure enough, there they came, laughing and having the best time. And, as always, there was Chad in the rear. He walked a little faster than usual. She fully expected him to burst into tears as soon as he got inside. His arms were empty, she noticed, and when the door opened she choked back the tears.

"Mommy has some cookies and milk for you," she said.

But he hardly heard her words. He just marched right on by, his face aglow, and all he could say was: "Not a one. Not a one."

Her heart sank.

And he added, "I didn't forget a one, not a single one!"

Turning Up Your Light

by Eric Allenbaugh

*M*ore than three decades ago, I was a sophomore at a large high school in Southern California. The student body of 3,200 was a melting pot of ethnic differences. The environment was tough. Knives, pipes, chains, brass knuckles and an occasional zip gun were commonplace. Fights and gang activity were weekly events.

After a football game in the fall of 1959, I left the bleachers with my girlfriend. As we walked down the crowded sidewalk, someone kicked me from behind. Turning around, I discovered the local gang, armed with brass knuckles. The first blow of the unprovoked attack immediately broke my nose, one of several bones to be broken in the pounding. Fists came from every direction as the fifteen gang members surrounded me. More injuries. A brain concussion. Internal bleeding. Eventually, I had to have surgery. My doctor told me that if I had been hit in the head one more time, I probably would have died. Fortunately, they did not harm my girlfriend.

After I recovered medically, some friends approached me and said, "Let's go get those guys!" That was the way problems were "resolved." After being attacked, evening the score became a priority. A part of me said, "Yes!" The sweet taste of revenge was clearly an option.

But another part of me paused and said no. Revenge did not work. Clearly, history had demonstrated time and again that reprisal only accelerates and intensifies conflict. We needed to do something differently to break the counterproductive chain of events.

Working with various ethnic groups, we put together what we called a "Brotherhood Committee" to work on enhancing racial relationships. I was amazed to learn how much interest fellow students had in building a brighter future. Not all bought into doing things differently. While small numbers of students, faculty and parents actively resisted these cross-cultural exchanges, more and more individuals joined in on the effort to make a positive difference.

Two years later, I ran for student body president. Even though I ran against two friends, one a football hero and the other a popular "big man on campus," a significant majority of the 3,200 students joined me in the process of doing things differently. I will not claim that the racial problems were fully resolved. We did, however, make significant progress in building bridges between cultures, learning how to talk with and relate to different ethnic groups, resolving differences without resorting to violence and learning how to build trust in the most difficult of circumstances. It's amazing what happens when people are on speaking terms with one another!

Being attacked by the gang those many years ago was clearly one of my toughest life moments. What I learned, however, about responding with love rather than returning hate has been a powerful force in my life. Turning up our light in the presence of those whose light is dim becomes the difference that makes the difference.

It's amazing what happens when people are on speaking terms with one another!

Summit America

by Lisa Manley

"Why me?" Todd screamed as his dad pulled his bloody body out of the murky lake and into the boat. Todd remained conscious as his father, two brothers and three friends sped to shore to get help.

It was all too surreal. Everyone had just spent a fun-filled day of water skiing at the lake in Oklahoma where his grandparents lived. Todd wanted to go inner-tubing after everyone finished water skiing. As he was untangling the ski ropes, the gears kicked into reverse and sucked his legs into the propellers, all in a flash of a moment. No one heard him scream until it was too late! Now he was in the hospital, hanging onto his life.

Both legs were severely injured. The sciatic nerve in his right leg had been severed, causing his leg to be permanently paralyzed from the knee down to his toes. The doctors said there was a chance he would never walk again. Todd slowly recovered from his wounds, but bone disease eventually set into his right foot. For the next seven years, he physically and emotionally battled to keep his leg. However, the time had finally come for him to face his biggest fear.

On a grim day in April, 1981, Todd lay conscious on the operating table at Massachusetts General waiting for the procedure to take place. He spoke calmly to the hospital staff about what kind of pizza he wanted to eat after the surgery. "I'd like Canadian bacon and pineapple," he joked. As the dreaded moment approached, a wave of calmness swept over him. Peace filled his heart as he thought of a Bible verse from his childhood, "Righteousness goes before him and prepares the way for his steps."

Todd knew with an unwavering conviction that his next step was to go through with the amputation. Any lingering doubt had vanished, and courage to face the inevitable prevailed. To obtain the lifestyle he desired, he had to lose his leg. In a few short minutes the leg was gone, but his whole future opened up.

He studied psychology at the suggestion of friends and family. He graduated magna cum laude, then took a job as clinical director of the Amputee Resource Center in Southern California. With his background in psychology and his personal experience as an amputee, he began to notice how he was able to inspire other amputees through his work.

"The steps I must take in my life are ordered," he remembered. "I guess I'm on the right path, but what is my next step?" he wondered.

Until the accident he led a normal life. He hiked, camped, played sports, flirted with girls and hung out with his buddies. After his injury, he continued to socialize with friends, but he had trouble playing sports. The artificial leg he received after the amputation allowed him to walk again, but not much more.

There were nights Todd would dream of running through grassy fields, only to wake up to the harsh reality of his situation. He desperately wanted to run again.

In 1993, he got his wish. A new type of prostheses, called a Flex-Foot, was developed. He acquired one through his prosthetist.

At first, he struggled to run, tripping over his feet and gasping for breath. However, with perseverance he was soon able to run twelve miles a day.

As he developed his abilities, a friend stumbled across an article in a magazine he thought Todd would find interesting. An organization was looking for an amputee to climb the highest mountain in each of the fifty states. There would be four other disabled climbers, and they would attempt to break a record by climbing all fifty highpoints in 100 days or less.

The idea excited Todd. *Why not go for it?* he thought. *I used to love to hike and now I have an opportunity to explore my limits.* He applied for the position and was immediately accepted.

The expedition was set to begin in April 1994. Todd had almost a year to get prepared. He began to train for the climb by working out daily, changing his diet and practicing rock climbing on weekends. Everyone agreed it was a good idea, but some thought it might not be the most responsible choice.

Todd didn't let those with negative concerns hold him back. He knew this was the right thing to do. When he prayed for direction, he was clear that this was to be the next step in his life.

Everything was working out perfectly — until February 1994, when he received some discouraging news. The funding for the expedition fell through. The project coordinator said he was sorry, but there was nothing left to do but disband the project.

"I will not quit!" Todd exclaimed. "I have put too much time and work into this to give up now. There is a message here that must be heard and, God willing, I'll find a way to make this expedition happen!"

Undaunted by the news, Todd set out to put the wheels in motion. During the next six weeks, he gathered enough financial support to get a new expedition under way. He garnered the support of a few friends to help him with the logistics of the climb. Whit Rambach would be his climbing partner, and I, Lisa Manley, would handle business from the home front. With everything now in order, he took off as scheduled with his new expedition called Summit America.

As Todd prepared for the expedition, he learned that only thirty-one people had ever reached the summit of all fifty highpoints. More people have successfully climbed Mount Everest, the highest mountain in the world.

Todd and Whit began the record for climbing all fifty highpoints at 5:10 P.M. on June 1, 1994, on Mount McKinley in Alaska. The previous record holder, Adrian Crane, and a military sergeant, Mike Vining, assisted them in their climb on Denali, the Indian name for Mount McKinley.

"The conditions on the mountain were extremely unpredictable," said Todd. "Storms could blow in within hours. It's like a game of cat and mouse trying to make it to the top.

"The weather got to minus 30 degrees

Fahrenheit at times," he said. "It took us twelve days to battle the weather, altitude sickness and the reality of the danger. I knew the mountain could be dangerous, but I didn't realize just how dangerous until two frozen bodies were being dragged down the mountain in front of me.

"It was one step at a time. The last thousand feet were the most difficult. I was taking three breaths for every step. I kept telling myself that my message would only be heard if I made it to the top. This realization propelled me to the summit."

The rest of the expedition was fast-paced and exciting. Hooked on Phonics came to Summit America's rescue by financing the rest of the climb. People took an interest in Todd, his determination to break the record, and his story. His message was being told in newspapers and on television and radio as he traveled around the country.

Everything was right on track until it was time to climb the forty-seventh highpoint, Mount Hood in Oregon. One week earlier, two people lost their lives on that mountain. Everyone advised Todd and Whit not to make the climb. They said it wasn't worth the risk.

Full of uncertainty and apprehension, Todd contacted his old high school friend and expert mountaineer, Fred Zalokar. When Fred heard his predicament, he said, "Todd, you've come too far to quit now. Fly me into town and I'm going to take you up that mountain—safely."

After a number of discussions with

mountain authorities and hours of careful planning, Todd, Whit and Fred successfully made it to the summit of Mount Hood. Now only three more highpoints stood between Todd and the record.

Then on August 7, 1994, at 11:57 A.M., Todd stood victorious at the peak of Hawaii's Mauna Kea. He had climbed all 50 high-points in just 66 days, 21 hours and 47 minutes, shattering the old climbing record by 35 days!

Even more remarkable, Todd was an amputee who shattered a record set by a man with two good legs.

Todd was elated, not only because he had set a new world climbing record, but because he now knew the answer to the question, "Why me?" that had haunted him ever since his accident at the lake.

At age thirty-three, he saw how this triumph over his tragedy could be used to encourage people everywhere. With a calm assurance he states, "Through faith in God and a belief in the abilities God gives you, you can overcome whatever challenges you face in life."

... he now knew the

answer to the question,

"Why me?"

Finding My Wings

by Sue Augustine

*L*ike so many girls, my self-confidence growing up was almost nonexistent. I doubted my abilities, had little faith in my potential and questioned my personal worth. If I achieved good grades, I believed that I was just lucky. Although I made friends easily, I worried that once they got to know me, the friendships wouldn't last. And when things went well, I thought I was just in the right place at the right time.

The choices I made reflected my self-image. While in my teens, I attracted a man with the same low self-esteem. In spite of his violent temper and an extremely rocky dating relationship, I decided to marry him. I still remember my dad whispering to me before walking me down the aisle, "It's not too late, Sue. You can change your mind." My family knew what a terrible mistake I was making. Within weeks, I knew it, too.

The physical abuse lasted for several years. I survived serious injuries, was covered with bruises much of the time and had to be hospitalized on numerous occasions. Life became a blur of police sirens, doctors' reports and family court appearances. Yet I continued to go back to the relationship, hoping that things would somehow improve.

After we had our two little girls, there were times when all that got me through the night was having those chubby little arms wrapped around my neck, pudgy cheeks pressed up against mine and precious toddler voices saying, "It's all right,

Mommy. Everything will be okay." But I knew that it wasn't going to be okay. I had to make changes — if not for myself, to protect my little girls.

Then something gave me the courage to change. Through work, I was able to attend a series of professional development seminars. In one, a presenter talked about turning dreams into realities. That was hard for me — even to dream about a better future. But something in the message made me listen.

She asked us to consider two powerful questions: "If you could be, do, or have anything in the world, and you knew it would be impossible to fail, what would you choose? And if you could create your ideal life, what would you dare to dream?" In that moment, my life began to change. I began to dream.

I imagined having the courage to move the children into an apartment of our own and start over. I pictured a better life for the girls and me. I dreamed about being an international motivational speaker so that I could inspire people the way the seminar leader had inspired me. I saw myself writing my story to encourage others.

So I went on to create a clear visual picture of my new success. I envisioned myself wearing a red business suit, carrying a leather briefcase and getting on an airplane. This was quite a stretch for me, since at the time I couldn't even afford a suit.

Yet I knew that if I was going to dream, it was important to fill in the details for my five senses. So I went to the leather store and modeled a briefcase in front of the mirror.

How would it look and feel? What does leather smell like? I tried on some red suits and even found a picture of a woman in a red suit, carrying a briefcase and getting on a plane. I hung the picture up where I could see it every day. It helped to keep the dream alive.

And soon the changes began. I moved the children to a small apartment. On only $98 a week, we ate a lot of peanut butter and drove an old jalopy. But for the first time, we felt free and safe. I worked hard at my sales career, all the time focusing on my "impossible dream."

Then one day I answered the phone, and the voice on the other end asked me to speak at the company's upcoming annual conference. I accepted, and my speech was a success. This led to a series of promotions, eventually to national sales trainer. I went on to develop my own speaking company and have traveled to many countries around the world. My "impossible dream" has become a reality.

I believe that all success begins with spreading your W.I.N.G.S.—believing in your worth, trusting your insight, nurturing yourself, having a goal and devising a personal strategy. And then, even impossible dreams become real.

"*If* you could be, do, or have anything in the world, and you knew it would be impossible to fail, what would you choose?"

Courage
in Action

by Bill Sanders

$\mathcal{A}$ couple of years ago, I witnessed courage that ran chills up and down my spine.

At a high school assembly, I had spoken about picking on people and how each of us has the ability to stand up for people instead of putting them down. Afterwards, we had a time when anyone could come out of the bleachers and speak into the microphone. Students could say thank you to someone who had helped them, and some people came up and did just that. A girl thanked some friends who had helped her through family troubles. A boy spoke of some people who had supported him during an emotionally difficult time.

Then a senior girl stood up. She stepped over to the microphone, pointed to the sophomore section and challenged her whole school. "Let's stop picking on that boy. Sure, he's different from us, but we are in this thing together. On the inside he's no different from us and needs our acceptance, love, compassion and approval. He needs a friend. Why do we continually brutalize him and put him down? I'm challenging this entire school to lighten up on him and give him a chance!"

All the time she shared, I had my back to the section where that boy sat, and I had no idea who he was. But obviously the school knew. I felt almost afraid to look at his section, thinking the boy must be red in the face, wanting to crawl under his seat and hide from the world. But as I glanced back, I saw a boy smiling from ear to ear. His whole body bounced up and down, and he raised one fist in the air. His body language said, "Thank you, thank you. Keep telling them. You saved my life today!"

We've Come a Long Way

by Pat Bonney Shepherd

*I*n 1996, we women are generally as solidly networking and supporting each other as our male counterparts have been for decades. It is a much friendlier place for women than it was forty or fifty years ago. Whenever I get complacent about that, I think about my mother—and I wonder if I could have survived what she went through back then.

By 1946, when my mother, Mary Silver, had been married to Walter Johnson for nearly seven years, she was the mother of four active, noisy children. I was the oldest, at nearly six; the others followed close behind: two boys, ages four and two, and then a girl, still just an infant. We lived in a very old house with no close neighbors.

I know little of my parents' lives at this time, but having raised two children myself in some remote corners of the country, I can imagine what it must have been like, especially for my mother. With four small children, a husband whose sense of obligation extended to bringing home the bacon and mowing the yard, no neighbors and almost no opportunities to develop any friends of her own, she had virtually no place to vent the intense pressures that must have built up in her. For some reason, my father decided that she was "straying." When she could possibly have found the time and whom she'd have been able to meet, let alone "stray" with, since the four of us were constantly underfoot, is a mystery to me. But my father made up his mind, and that was that.

One early spring day in 1946, my mother left the house to get milk for the baby. When she came back, my father was standing at an upstairs window with a gun. He said, "Mary, if you try to come into this house, I'll shoot your children." That was how he let her know that he was suing her for divorce.

That was the last time my mother ever saw that house. She was forced to walk away with only the clothes she was wearing and the money in her purse—and a quart of milk. Today, she would probably have options: a local shelter, an 800 number to call, a network of friends she had developed through a full- or part-time job. She'd have a checkbook and credit cards in her pocket. And she could turn without shame to her family for support. But in 1946, she had none of that. Married people just didn't get divorced.

So there she was — completely alone. My father had actually managed to turn her own father against her. Now my grandfather forbade my grandmother to speak to her daughter when her daughter needed her most.

At some point before they went to court, my father contacted her and said: "Look, Mary, I don't really want a divorce. I only did all this to teach you a lesson." But my mother could see that bad though her situation was, it was preferable to going back to my father and letting him raise us kids. So she said in effect, "No way. I've come this far, there's no going back."

Where could she go? There was no going home. She couldn't stay there in Amherst, first because she knew no one would take her in; second, because with the returning GIs there would be no hope of work for her; and finally, and most important, because my father was there. So she got on a bus to the only place that held any hope for her—New York City.

My mother had one thing going for her: She was well educated, with a degree in mathematics from Mt. Holyoke College. But she had taken the usual route of women in the 1930s and '40s: She had gone directly from high school to college to marriage. She had no idea how to find work and support herself.

New York City had several things in its favor: It was only 200 miles away, so she could afford a bus ticket, and it was a big city, so there had to be a job hiding there somewhere. She absolutely had to find a way to support all four of us kids. Upon arriving in New York, she located a YWCA where she could stay for $1.50 a night. There was a Horn & Hardart Automat nearby where she could put nickels into slots next to windows with food behind them, and for about $1 a day, feed herself egg salad sandwiches and coffee. Next she started pounding the streets.

For several days, which became several weeks, she found nothing: no jobs for math majors, male or female, no jobs for women at all. Each night she went back to the Y, washed out her underwear and her white blouse, hung them to dry, and in the morning used the Y's iron and ironing board to press the wrinkles out of the blouse. These items, along with a gray flannel skirt, constituted her entire wardrobe. Caring for them took up a portion of the long evening she faced alone at the Y. With no books, no extra nickels or dimes for a newspaper, no telephone (and no one to call if she'd had one), and no radio except downstairs (where the Y guest list was somewhat frightening), the nights must have been truly awful.

Predictably, her money dwindled, as did the list of employment agencies. It came down finally to a particular Thursday, the last employment agency in the city, and less in her pocket than the $1.50 she needed for that night's lodging. She was trying very hard not to think about spending the night in the street.

She trudged up several flights of stairs to

reach the agency, filled out the obligatory forms, and when it was her turn to be interviewed, steeled herself for the bad news. "We're really sorry, but we don't have anything for you. We hardly have jobs enough for the men we have to place." For, of course, the men came first for any available jobs.

My mother felt nothing as she rose from her chair and turned to the door. Numb as she was, she was almost out the door before she realized the woman had mumbled something else.

"I'm sorry, I missed that. What did you say?" she asked.

"Well, I said there's always George B. Buck & Company but nobody ever wants that job. Nobody ever stays there," the woman repeated, nodding her head toward a box of file cards on top of a nearby cabinet.

"What is it? Tell me about it," my mother said anxiously, sitting back down in the wooden chair. "I'll take anything. When does it start?"

"Well, it's a job as an actuarial clerk, which you're qualified for, but the pay's not good and I'm sure you wouldn't like it," said the agent, pulling the relevant card out of the file box. "Let's see, it says here that you can start anytime. I suppose that means you could go down there now. The morning's not too far gone."

My mother says she literally snatched the card from the agent's hand and ran down the stairs. She didn't even stop to catch her breath as she ran the several blocks to the address listed on the card. When she presented herself to the surprised personnel manager, he decided that she could indeed start work that very morning if she wanted to—there was plenty to do. And it turned out that Thursday was payday. Back in those days, most companies paid their employees out of the till for time worked up to and including payday itself — so, miraculously, when five o'clock came, she was handed cash for the five hours she had worked that very day. It wasn't much, but it got her through to the next Thursday, and then the next, and so on.

May Silver Johnson remained with George B. Buck & Company for thirty-eight years, rising to a position of great respect in the company. I remember she had a corner office — no mean feat in downtown Manhattan.

After she'd been there ten years, she was able to buy us a house in suburban New Jersey, half a block from a bus to the city.

These days, every second household seems to be headed by a working single mother, and it is easy to forget that there was once a time that such a life was almost unthinkable. I am both humbled to reflect on my mother's accomplishments and proud enough to bust my buttons! If I've come a long way, baby, it's because I was carried a large part of that way by the efforts of many, many other women before me — with this remarkable woman, my mother, leading the way.

One for the Team

by Kim Noone

This story was told by an old priest one Sunday. It is a true story of when he served in the military.

One day their drill sergeant came out and threw a hand grenade into a group of young soldiers. The men all ran away and took cover away from the grenade. Then the drill sergeant told them that the grenade was not set to explode and he just did it to see their reaction. The next day a newly recruited soldier joined the group. The drill sergeant told the other soldiers not to tell the new soldier what was going to happen. As the drill sergeant came out and threw the grenade into the crowd of soldiers, the new soldier, not knowing it wasn't going to explode, threw himself on top of the grenade to prevent it from killing the other men. He was willing to die for his fellow soldiers.

That year the young man was awarded the only medal for courage and bravery that had not been won during battle.

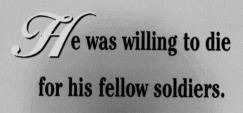

He was willing to die

for his fellow soldiers.